I0643786

BOOKWORMS

Our World of Water

Bayous

Arthur Best

Cavendish Square
New York

Published in 2018 by Cavendish Square Publishing, LLC
243 5th Avenue, Suite 136, New York, NY 10016

First Edition

Library of Congress Cataloging-in-Publication Data

Names: Best, Arthur, author.
Title: Bayous / Arthur Best.
Description: New York : Cavendish Square Publishing, [2018] | Series: Our World of Water | Includes index.
Identifiers: LCCN 2017022534 (print) | LCCN 2017025759 (ebook) | ISBN 9781502630896 (E-book) | ISBN 9781502630865 (Paperback) | ISBN 9781502630872 (6 pack) | ISBN 9781502630889 (Library bound)
Subjects: LCSH: Bayous--Juvenile literature.
Classification: LCC GB1203.8 (ebook) | LCC GB1203.8 .B468 2018 (print) | DDC 551.48/3--dc23
LC record available at https://lccn.loc.gov/2017022534

Editorial Director: David McNamara
Copy Editor: Nathan Heidelberger
Associate Art Director: Amy Greenan
Designer: Alan Sliwinski
Production Coordinator: Karol Szymczuk
Photo Research: J8 Media

The photographs in this book are used by permission and through the courtesy of: Cover David Kozlowski/Getty Images; p. 5 Olivier Cirendini/Lonlely Planet Images/Getty Images; p. 7 Philip Gould/Corbis/Getty Images; p. 9 EdwinM/Shutterstock.com; p. 11 IrinaK/Shutterstock.com; p. 13 Sandy Huffaker/Getty Images; p. 15 ZakiraZ/Shutterstock.com; p. 17 Moelyn Photos/Moment/Getty Images; p. 19 Radius Images/Alamy Stock Photo; p. 21 Oneinchpunch/Shutterstock.com.

Printed in the United States of America

Contents

Bayous are like swamps.

They are made by rivers.

The water moves very slowly.

Bayous are near **coasts**.

The land is very flat.

Water from the sea can enter bayous.

LADY LUCY

Trees live in bayous.

They can live in the water.

Other plants live above the water.

Moss can hang from trees!

Bayous have many animals.

Shrimp live in bayous.

People catch them to eat.

Many birds live in bayous.

They can catch fish.

Alligators live in bayous.

So do some snakes that can swim!

Bayous are special places.

There are not many on Earth.

People visit bayous.

They take special boats!

New Words

bayous (BY-ooz) Places where water moves slowly.

coasts (COHSTS) Places where the sea meets the land.

moss (MOSS) A small, soft plant.

shrimp (SHRIMP) A small water animal people can eat.

Index

About the Author

Arthur Best lives in Wisconsin with his wife and son. He has written many other books for children. He has seen bayous in Louisiana.

About BOOKWORMS

Bookworms help independent readers gain reading confidence through high-frequency words, simple sentences, and strong picture/text support. Each book explores a concept that helps children relate what they read to the world they live in.